CLARK COOLIDGE

ON THE NAMEWAYS

VOLUME TWO

THE FIGURES • 2001

The author thanks the editors of the following magazines
in which some of these poems first appeared: *The Blind See
Only This World: Poems for John Wieners* (Granary Books/Pressed Wafer),
Blue Book, *The Gig*, *The Hat*, *Lingo 8 Pulp Poetry Supplement*, *Prosodia*,
Shiny and *Skanky Possum*.

The publisher wishes to thank the Saul Rosen Foundation for generous
and continued support.

Typesetting & design by SAILING AFTER LUNCH
The Figures, 5 Castle Hill Ave. Great Barrington, MA 01230
Distributed by SPD, Berkeley, CA

Copyright © 2001 by Clark Coolidge
ISBN 1-930589-07-7

CONTENTS

Arsenic and Old Blemishes 11
The Meat Statement 12
Weapons of Mere Distraction 13
Hey I'm Fragmentary 14
Flashed from the Baritone Manual 15
Some Corpuscular Travelers 16
Your Skin's in Danger (Sicky) 17
A Ruffled Sheen 18
Golly Stoppers 20
Carpet Matters 21
Electroman Finishes 22
Prelude to a Flapjack 23
Looking If Not Lasting 24
Bells of the Squimp 25
An Extra Tong for the Salt Match 26
Just Like a Western to Pretend 27
The Bark to Roll 28
Night of the Sugar Shake Shot 29
The Diorite Man 30
Gas Propeller Found 31
The Edicts of Belly Filmus 32
Blown Stack (A Counter) 33
A Further 34
Grampus Bows 35
Medals on the Old Rubber Hat 36
The Lip It's Being Brought Off 38
Brian Likes the Avenue 39
Those the Coughing Sisters? 40
Nick Diabase 41
The Story That Was Waiting/At Haunted Cellar Station ..42

Sails of the Temperature Dopester 43
The Hero's Lanolin 44
Okey Dokey Mister Condu 45
The Shout As Far As Washington 46
The Ogilvie Unit 47
Groan If You Like 48
Displacement (Encouragement) 49
Gandolphus Replay 50
Garva States It 51
The Cockroach is Missing 52
Night Has Its Loads 54
Though It Stang 55
Bastards Came 56
Zapper Cleanse 57
These Are the Louder Droppings 58
Nary an Oater 59
Chance Moves Out 60
Blown Cues in Wild Woods 61
Moo Goo Gai Penury 62
The Gill Rows to Nowhere 63
Cheep 64
Cause Cap's the Limit 65
A Banana Tuck in the Moon (Varlet) 66
Huey Louie and Dewey on Eggs 67
Low on the Moniker (It Arrives in Waves) 68
The Deros 69
A Treater's Crossups 70
Ways to Form in Time (The Blinkers) 71
And the Lunatic Rotate 72
Overnovel Owls Bearing Down 73
Every Deep Has Lower Developments 74
Some Early Canon 75

Stretched Out Till the Knowledge Stops 77
I Found an Elegy 78
Bactine's Famous Flameout 79
Must You? (Saw) 80
Steamboat Springs for the Night 1965 81
Apportionment and Suspended Ending 82
Load Soft, He Might Tumble .83
Plus Nine Lines of Fear 84
More Helpings of the Vital Roster 85
Of the Brighter Buyer 87
With the Plasticity of Fools 88
Gone Over 89
Glad to See You Standing 90
Short of Nowhere 91
Tabs on Glitter 92
One Shape Returns 93
Rhonda Fleming at the Medicine Building 94
Lights Only the One Time 95
Mother to Mount My Tree 96
Lawn Lawyer Heaven 98
Into the Gum Again and He's Mean 99
Every Man Jack Chews It Over (Green) 100
Gulp 101
The Gunsel Loses (Set Your Phasers on Disturb) 102
I Blew Eisenhower's Dick Off 103
Surgery in Friends 104
On the Prod 105
Flavor of the Mouth 106
Bauxite on the Books 107
Draw Me a Short Deer 108
Mamacita Pops a Ligature 109
The Sneeze in Profile 110

Butter Up Your Entropy/While the Smiles Are Free 111
The Metal Petals' Creamy Reach 112
Like a Kneeflex 113
Braniac on Banjo 114
In Bruceman's Batteryway 115
Tell Me One Thing 116
Trying 117
Cup Rings 118
Back in the Time of the Tube 119
Trapped in a Nazi Stoop 120
Not Oh 121
Are You Ashamed of Your Sulfur? 122
Outward Till You Duck 123
Men Without Labels 124
Others 125
In Memory of the Undead 126
Darlings Bound 127
Like the Blisters on a Piece of Champagne 128

On the Nameways

Volume Two

ARSENIC AND OLD BLEMISHES

I live in America
Uncle, wait for the coin to drop
what do I know about
Arizona maybe?
Jack Warden muscles in
Arbuthnot the Gremlin sings
I don't have to wash again
Antonin Artaud in his shoulderpads
leave and you can say hello
a whole hill of muffins with no oil
just butterpeas
Barnaby had no shellac on his balls
how are you with wings?
the blossoming of certain kinds
can douse thought and go among?
Adelle made an admirable tea
not to bang it on the door to a train
would you shove Avalon aside
like a shawl?
I prefer Ken Stanton
all in a picture's vibration
Karl Malden in the moral void
a battle of stake and recalcitrance
but Benny Benefactor died
closeness? I wouldn't credit it
a nut soup on Sunny Innings Day
and only a single patent leather hair

THE MEAT STATEMENT

Look out! Needs!
and here comes Steve Buscemi
on a ringtail cat
till some of us have parroted
our last
and rim to rim the proper fills
are formed
is this a matter of garcon
bring me my ticker?
or did the Olive Goons devolve
still further?
last night there was a spent
match at my place
a sure sign of sound
and terrible advice
with malingers and everyone stupid
planning bygone escapades
I have scored my screen
I have watched that vanilla
pumping
get off me, Calloway
I have chased the last of me

WEAPONS OF MERE DISTRACTION

All the money in the meters of Los Angeles
wouldn't
consult the Changs they're okay
at the Apple Sutra Karma Factory
red candy dangles
I found myself chasing
out of twine out of eye
the crux of a duck
Matt Strange my cousin here trembles
tracked enough so all can tell
his mumbles are treasures
the spongework between what happens
"I don't *have* the Mars Bar"
Muddy Waters says Halt!
there are runes where once was soup
or a more ignorant barrister
with patriotic lesions
or parasitic lighting I'm not sure
but raise your lifestyle belts anyway
the better lessons are coming

HEY I'M FRAGMENTARY

You're lying to me about the turmeric
no? try 3-B
siddown! now I'm ready
Tweedledum between the wars
are you fraught? I'm a dunce
so be sure of nothing
notes on radiator drapes and pulls
have you ever taken coffees?
try Napalm Airlines
not any New York in a gunnysack
that ape from Singapore
right away they want to take your number
I'm a big dumb Abner-type dude
lost in apple space
a dangerous mental statement
one of the ones with no eyes
and won't put off ailments
the last time I washed myself in public
Buicks

FLASHED FROM THE BARITONE MANUAL

Great purple suns rustling in the pumice
this Xmas
we're ventrified in fossil peels
granted a few whiffs of the alkali
who is this Hiram Blender?
and what is his invention for doing?
blasphemous the tree house
the neighbors bought
but I could pass it like a phlegm
you know your guitar?
which petrifies in the Flemish Bunker
red tail and head
the fisher presence dead
and all over the states
this sickish health
an apple for your bath

SOME CORPUSCULAR TRAVELERS

Pick the turnpaste local balloon
Stymy
and haggle only so far as
your lozenges will hold
Trumpetina
Patriot of Joy
and highway amplitude
the worst record store in
existence could tell you that
the toad'll want his spoons back
as soon as you'll die
and even Neotyners have wants
stumped as even trees do get
I'm living the life
smooth as a porch
the spryest winkers come past
kneel as you watch
just come along alone
and I'll put you with some stars
only so far as they've gone
out of style
the doorway's out of oil
the treadmill's out of cattle
signed Normid Nemo
age none

YOUR SKIN'S IN DANGER (SICKY)

Laocöon moves at lariat speed
a floating flex of fog horn
gummy bears later and tag-alongs
all gone out of the knot
"I ain't got any" he gargles
and the kids lick and lap
canned in such stringless space
this story needs a pedestal
"and I *got* one"
Laocöon on oxygen
and spare planetary system
"my beard's been spotted"
but such clods are tangles

A RUFFLED SHEEN
after Wieners

The Gurrelieder of Charlie Parker
boiling up to a crispness
a cheapness of lostness I encounter
the Hucklebuck
and the latrine I'll never wear again
wrist rested on marble block
the Exorcist caught a treeload of
there is laughter and there is putty
oh old gold blanker go with me now
I'd never look over *that* shoulder
those gold glasses a case of back braces
seam of frond and the ten-man stallions
know what it's like
let's take a pile for our trouble
a franking life full of bags and boxes
and a tilling of the blokes Lynch says
panties and death are the same
let's swim awful for your hands
to be thrown out as I walk worth saving
Sarah Pictures my stormgiven friend
Predusil my epigone staggers on the land

Breathland between the rungs
a solid saliva keeps them there
a fly may be fancier but your window knocker
blonde cavortrist embellishing and wavering
from the top of this knob I sight
the central premise

Ostragod has a terrible head
a mottled brick for a tail
and there is no greater farmer than presence
or a far family shirt
or the Wallwalker Plantagenet
Shropshire or no Hobbyknot
I see things sinking in the pushing traffics
accelerate till you hit Marge
those who have nothing but this bubble to love
out of the mendicant's very own pen
perspire knock off and masturbate
take it in its own telling
a buffalo flaunt and miles of mice
poor heating in the larval dome misspent
he'll have no harm come to it
him of the coal drawn home
I just want anything away from everything
do you hear me, Percepied?
just make sure you cut a path
to the bathroom, Marston
but then Pan Harris I always could
lick liquid lips
mid tulgey fears
and the kraken wakes
as the Dead budge among us
he was a hydrofool that crud with the helmet
I couldn't gun him higher than Tex his lighter
Trudy her double drawers
the cement scene with the hack
the pilot trundling back
even the masked creaks at the very end
were in tempo!

GOLLY STOPPERS

Crawling around in Arctic strangeness
under the little bubble roofs
barking our heads our lunatic pates
I'd have to learn to follow
a hamadryad
ensconced in a field with her
with three legions and a tarmac
to believe in
far from any ability to sue
with a rag on the back
no stunts so no lints
only a streamer for the suitcase
they bunked Palo Alto down in
it was an orange hamadryad
whose pumpkins had come loose

CARPET MATTERS

The dream had me in houses
on the road
on the hard way to seemingly
the boxes said in-town movies
glanced past these weapons in fun
past heat vent populations
and formers of the grub
had a heck of an aerodrome
in herringbone
so the last laugh was larval
on the way to where frankly
the only good receiver's a refrigerator
and the animals all stain in rows
so be a good human and drive me
a friend just to hold up this end be
a jammer and only then send

ELECTROMAN FINISHES

An ExLax carrier I want to be
an extraveler with hint of career
a gold intentional travesty at the interval
my hidden knowledge applied to the world's seal
guts relayed by barograph
lumpen peels
daft
I have looked beyond myself and found an acre
composed as a pin

PRELUDE TO A FLAPJACK

Granite papers are limited
only by the ducks they attract
Fotheringill nodded at a page of
his flatters on fire
the lapel was furnace but
no one knew the boy
outlived his dulcets and puffery
so go on would you?
the rubber pony was enough of a phony
who could afford to use Yeltsin neat?
crust before it made a diff and when
varlets lapsed back into cartridge snap
Granite limped less one payload
and Tromper he listened and made the ducks
jump and pen a new Magna Vox
thus had we the sodium
paid,
        The Pallor

LOOKING IF NOT LASTING

A house that was a hose-sider
one with nailer notches
the waffle known as pink and green
or you have mountains in the distance
robots with blotters
I see the next house but one
it had many side enfoldments of
place where the head isn't swayed
too late for looking up at the lake
it was a drama major puddle razzer
banana-loose and pretty soon ducking
that handled those paints
in lots of frontal masking known
as the Hues of the Nephews
nothing will stop *them* from coming

BELLS OF THE SQUIMP

I'm coming! screamed the Fireman
as the Warden announced my thoughts on deck
stone cut sheets spun to a bagginess me
Placenta was the murmur
the next member Chas Fambrough
for what wag has forgotten him?
nearly
the pot contained clear ones
hand dabs the looser till
the Fright Cunts come clear away
Welcome to the Stoving of the Bruce
inclined to dish position anyway
as the triremes turn sirens
and everybody blabs along
even the hung ones on the treat map
might be earwigs or scoundrels
inching up the post with a flattery of sores
core poles from the spice-dosed East
and my captain was Marlin
you know how close comes everything else
even the standby goalie had water wings
pencil lungs
all the Corbetts were laughing
even the leatherette ones

AN EXTRA TONG FOR THE SALT MATCH

The McCoy Tyner device on your
joystick will release grey
matter if you make a mistake
indictment pending for brute frames
dropping pent eggs
stacking all down the delta to
Pyewacket and the slaveries of both ends
it enters mass malarky
but bigger than your house can save the day
Tynerism has paid out into
Europes of the fatal edge
industrial replays and a tensing of
the heavy water bribes
there's so much more meat to be played
till an adept of the horizontal
moon takes his place
high on the revolving suitcase
we'll have to prane and dulge
finger a pan switch
and stipulate styles
prone till the Mohorovici Replay
and reshelling of the headliner pennies
you might even hear him miss

JUST LIKE A WESTERN TO PRETEND

Naked pig farmer shakes his wand
and poof! a lot of us are gone
this is the American Jugular
way low down
only three more pulls of your watch to come
nimble as a rake with attachments
'cause it's only a habit
push pull the rules of a fool
and I'd fly if I'd lost
a few less moments
sky's the garment
there's just no stopping some turns
of the plan
of the lead of the land

THE BARK TO ROLL

The Emetic sails at dawn
the Septic's sails are torn
the vascular is born
tremens
the bird with no neck to peck
got lost in these waves
grounded
they say the pale are fatal
Borax or Bust
so I turn over and go to sea
on a peep on a mere
balance beam in the Unguentine Swells
where the laughter
where the doom is concentric
just bare those sails

NIGHT OF THE SUGAR SHAKE SHOT

Evidently that orifice is not hungry
are there any till queasiness takes over?
just that the cat is licking the plastic
off her face
double you
like a trophy buckled to the ceiling
now who or what is Claude?
distant old clods in the Christmas attic
Gandolfo's Reflex
comes in Nicky of the Cold Cop Lights
screams goals
Funny Face had a bloody farming habit
on our old phone but lacks a shimmy pin
Peter Jesus gone green on stairs
the search party found a little
girdle in the park
"now hear me out!"
just like having a wart removed
we've gone all sticky with hope here
find yourself a kneehole

THE DIORITE MAN

A sort of small blob of personality
and a pistol on the sink
he won't do it
has to load up his pet with stories
hears that Art Pepper has lost all hope
puts his fury where his pencil is
nothing in the ceiling but photons
he talks of a carcinoma misplaced
the choice impervious to fear
there's a rum tit waiting in
the glossular vapor car
he made nothing on
pretend to be helping when you
cross those wires
and so an earthquake
but that was across the street
he was the neighbor you nearly
wished you had
a vital sign of our times: he's
suburban master of the lunar canyons
don't forget the combinations
all taking place behind gas
slab sober and sized-up like
a plant without windows
or salty pearls by Daisetz Malarky
his pollution brand
his side of the slam grand
lithic signs of the kalimbic system

GAS PROPELLER FOUND

Grodin recapped his hirelings
for they were slant
front
breached if not watched
a pepper mill it was
bleeding for care and torture
a godling in a pen atwitch
was marvelous and staid
Grodin stood at the top of the room
grinning like Electricman
in the spread position
held to a set of locked teeth
and there was no further breathing

THE EDICTS OF BELLY FILMUS

Some days the old cuckoo has me
up for lessons
tame enough to blow
the cereal off the door
the stretchings off the floor
in hall and terrace pouchy slivers
it's a mass land cape
only a mile till Morpo blows
we have subsidies
has the fault settled its board
sides on call?
a movie histamine muddled
the age of these areas
call Throckmorton
kill that arrow
about to do a favor but
Moon Swamp slipped
an orbit all out in irises
till the novenas came in dull
but we'll prove futurity
on a rock spent
with Doras and Aprils and Caspians
rooting for the last ones
their 'brellas and spongebreath taints
the school board that never rants
"why the scope of our problems"
signed the Devil
with his shovel

BLOWN STACK (A COUNTER)

The trouble with cunts is
they repaint too easily
the smile comes off and
the varnish stays
how many bottles?
who can stem all
these comic viaducts?
like tar peeling off
the bridge of your mouth
it's done and you're out
revealed as diamonds in rain
a patch of the vein exposed
and all the little clips of
a choppy sentience
try reaching for a frond
get a load of my hand
go off in your head
the Gandy Divers ensconced
in red lead

A FURTHER

Whee, roses!
the whole country as if a robe
before us
spun grapes sprung horses
a northern hole in which to dwell
smoke of hornitos
bramblemen
and hostelry savages
as one clawn bone on a moon
a hill of spines
tin pot of sphinxes
capitulary dogs
the people march in clouds
I have seen the organs pushing up
the organs of stone
and mountains full of bells
and victuals out of ice
and tension humps and mongery
we will spread further
we will haul that burger
and eat it before the spice halls drain
in brevity waivers
no one to gain the lamp
all numbered and shined by
the Marshals of Shod

GRAMPUS BOWS

Astrid Gilberto and Frankie Gilbane
got married in the navy yard rain
and so all things do come to an end?
streaked shot of those crayon benders
"Christ, a fault in the Grand Canyon!"
have they ever say opened the drapes to see?
rather leather a dog to a tree
carcinomic vitamins are happening
but in the film of a starbody
some ribbons still flow at the end
there is no end
the marriage took place in full view
of a steer
their carbons found in a shoe
"we had plans"

MEDALS ON THE OLD RUBBER HAT

The Gypsies were playing as usual
the Perry Mason Theme in a backyard

I'm afraid it's not possible
not undercover not a whisker

the plan was to see if romance would cover it
I would not let such a light leave the building

lets go in a minute a brute coffee stain
a brain so dark I can never get away

over there is the picture of fire
on the terrace of no respect

I took a souvenir of her grotesque inanity
had it enlarged and never returned

is it better? say yes
give me a hand with the room's glass residue

its prisoner had built up a huge vocabulary
mountains bullets apricots and ovals

then the shit hit his hand
the word for cat removed from the language

and began to read with the fire of a peppermint
stroke on stroke till the interment was over

but the nature of the final argument
which is merely to describe disrobe

it only stretches from head to neck
these thoughts these eye-openings

give me quantity give me latitude
the fools along the way will show up

then the sun blinks certain death
a certain health rubbed raw with shade

and the yelling like a jelly rolled on
like the shaper of days

arrow music plays
pales

THE LIP IT'S BEING BROUGHT OFF

Orpiment dens
niter dripping from the points
radishes in toto
these comprise our city
anything for hire anytime
every night it's tip up the map
fall home with the radiolarians
condenser juice of Margaret Whiting
and the one standing with
his back to the fruit-lit plant
bless our handled planet
fill our homes with these animalcules
hail dish city

BRIAN LIKES THE AVENUE

Corduroy deeps
and the anvil stirs
he's not to inhabit it says
his face is the one
his coffin replaces
seeds with eyes
have we had to overlaugh a little?
smallish sideshow down by the sand dump
where the kids play with liquids nights
Mrs. Solly trembles
it's not pugnacious to be feeling
out the core before it reaches
the center of Tiny Town
a cloth torn clown recommences
the hobby horn that slips our latch
breeds shenanigans   don't cough
it's only a town gone off duty

THOSE THE COUGHING SISTERS?

And lumps for sakes
the stocking dressing
stamps and poll results
hostilities till the horn
then tot up your sessions
we're the Children of Corn
cops of muscles and adders
treat back from ample visits
fatal sound on a trumpet
board load to the simplet
and Gordo comes and makes
the birds all replace each other
like elves grown craven
these crows must be stuffed
let's dig in the buff
this Prattler on Avon

NICK DIABASE

Went keenly mental on the desperate world
there we are watched from all sides
why pay knuckles?
in this beatnik blow man funny
should we walk into the womb?
I have knock money
known for perhapsishness
Diabase waltzes in through two dim walls
a tuck slicing back where the sidemen form
there's no number on your amounting to anything
Nick rides the tin core of airplanes
monstrous to a fuss
got that girlycorn in your hand?
breadboard's all this meal turns into
small as the vase on your price
she can't act
so's your sister
I can't come back for the dive
but Diabase has his way
with a crock and this Chevy
grown element-heavy

THE STORY THAT WAS WAITING
AT HAUNTED CELLAR STAION

I farted
with violence within
ounces of the tin street
a matter of Tom Mix hitching
the thought to the dream
of molecules torn and watered
the lid from the ice and the
quarter ship rolling
it's beginning to show
Francis the Talking Card
cuffs on the yellowing history
claps to come and the onions
of the blessing
I only wish I had ordered
that and the corridor
to the depths of unfastening
that pipe swing
your ordinary wing

SAILS OF A TEMPERATURE DOPESTER

Along the Tigger Rows
and down among the bunkum beads and geodes
one with a name of sweat
I'd have to fall by to find Curly
former mayor of a whole street
where they shivered from subgum tax
teller lines and Vigaro
heard the throats of those beasts?
I drew a curtain not designer sheets
stint of the shirts
it was a left turn onto Cider Row
the place of the boy with no hands
corporate wings in woods of no lights
where the undertow of gold hope's
drawn by a hauser rope
and we thrill and flee
"no!"

THE HERO'S LANOLIN

Down a long dreaded avenue
shelf
in the felt distance the Cathedral
of the Sockets
but the ancient hero had a cowboy
shirt
breaks his bike out in bushes
the whole goddam tone of the time
garden stalactites
onyx pressed under the hood
she is a woman with a head
short of her handlers
"you look tired you must be happy"
crap
"can't focus on the bong in her face"
dolt
a starlit barn but it's merely holes
a blue barrier open
the blue barrier tutti amici here
so to come on get in here
borracho   hides
but all these mean men mean to be true
or sick during the Opera of the Broken Wagons
the green covered over and he was stumped
just so long as the nut can be crushed
the bridge ensnared and the train
totalled out
and the moon comes into the house
to live

OKEY DOKEY MISTER CONDU

Bruise trails on the sunset
dock at my knee
bring me my Postum
at least look and see
a treat to have my pesters
all wrapped
floral in visit and conked
at the wrist
his other name was Bolio
frosted as a wicket
the Blown Guys shouldered
at the castle
they are about eights and nine
lengths of butt pipe
you got your revenant bolts
and fricassees of the pith?
bulbs in all the known bowls
and oxygen where it twitched?
you won't know a dolt from
its bow
and then the casters light
their mercy lips and the tin
grove turns to smither
how many well dug nights?
how many churlies of the center?
how will you bag your mother?
bleed your calling on a card?

THE SHOUT AS FAR AS WASHINGTON

When Gordo tried to seize the tightpost
night came quick to shut him
"to please all you Palookas I'd
edge away from anything"
go to salsa go to high
the cable math has been done in stealth
hogans contain more coffee if you latch 'em
and the cold pod hangs at the captain's beck
to come make loops then duck
the animals seize up
a vial or two of blind sense for real
"will those with cabins go to them now?"
that cardigan over the mouth
saved the cow

THE OGILVIE UNIT

Kept their trash to Sundays
other days Walnetto Surprise
one had sapphire eyes
another would be so bold as
to sit out fires
the spell of the nautical launch
the telemetry ditch
a call goes out for small aids
see the group had thought
the hammer already thrown
the beach cleared of fuzz
the overnite diner
so all repaired to Blinstrub's
cocky as a lamer
Silurian sort of veteran
one that's never lost his
cheese credits free plaudits
then half a lung came open
and the boys from Dog Palace
dug and did favors
"we all colored the home"
the hardest part being the barn

GROAN IF YOU LIKE

Fire stained his eyes like futures
whole trees landing in his lap
forepate alight with societal plugs
it was a mystery how
the school came up with a plan
pus in the walls
so many trips to the lumber attics
where the whiny stacked like sirens
four to a pod
in a ten liquor pen
it was nothing to be taught
but there was leather at the back
like her hair was tied
spaced to the teeth as if trotting
that whole year was mileage
a pure direction to be pumping with
nobody saved their shovels

DISPLACEMENT (ENCOURAGEMENT)

The washout came when his head
fell off
body out of whack
a longer pair of jeans
and the advice from Driver Prim
stall
he'd been having belt wick problems
a yellowish roughness by half
that and the stuff with potatoes
thought he could last till Wednesday
but the stovepipe wouldn't
then his clothes came up
and the horrible plot with
piano roll backing
he was trembling
though sending
rotting from the core
blebs and blobs here and there
from the almost constant venting
we couldn't imagine he'd budge
but that's the thing with porn singers
they bulge
given certain limited hatchings
and the calm rooms that contain them
not to mention their rugs

GANDOLPHUS REPLAY

In a blooming Hejira
I tried twenty times
to inculcate snarls
it was Colgate Summer
and suddenly pathetic
with the damage on the inside
but three windows wide and
as if a ditch had spoken open
you got a hobby notion of it all by now?
whose only greeting smells
the coughing replacement was jewels
top of the cork to you
and the lifting of anything small
there was even a moment when the highway
to Calipha gained a pole
and then the boils came strolling

GARVA STATES IT

These ones had spent their summer
being mold sitters
no matter how you shave it
it bells the fraud
but the linkages come up feelers
internal to spall and meld
I know, I'm Gumby
player of the full glance small plane
the day the wave wound up
one more placement of track
pumpkin outfits and cylindrical
branding 'round the something can
the brindle win
the origin of all stopping for
the skin

THE COCKROACH IS MISSING

A fantastic planet
with nuts on it
attain to an almost
perfect flatulence
sound and remembering the brain
under investigation for its practices
as a separate country
dull as a pestered imagination
"let's go scurvy on it"
or pianissimo fire wad
meanwhile Brain #25
never leaves the field
autosuggestion in its own shell
strictly pumpkin or pumpgun
"quit chewing in my ear"
he was a member of the Locket Squad
peremptory barn plasm
but I'll remember the windows
nodes and sentry places in the skull
reach for your shenanigans
proctologist waiting
a desperate man shoveling
or is he snorkeling? he's bubbling
his head has become quite a fixture
attention Conqueror Worm
"just leave me off at the dome"
grunts and plays all the better numbers
grounds of the run-on nations

ends disassembling the planet by halves
antennae caught in the same switches
antlers in a treetop sale

NIGHT HAS ITS LOADS

The scrabblers with snow
had their own ideas about how things
were supposed to shove
close to a dinger
the way it holds
the shovelers of toast
drew their notions from Brace Beamer
land on the sun then
hunch on the vine
it was a bleat of roses
collected as damp in the houses
the gogglers of boast knew
and fangled on it
as if a lit stone
scandled in twain hung
puffing to pick you up

THOUGH IT STANG

Twenty miles of barbecue wire
fits them to the padded fountains
it's so hot out in day and they wish
the tongs of the funnies were padlocked
another summer of grinding relays
sharks to the optimum and overages
turn out the lights on your tree farm
hold over those matches till Halloween
for all that quit it will be fun
watching their backs come unlatched
hearing them march before the stars
go home like none of these
stunts are in parallel
none of the sideshows going

BASTARDS CAME

Lucky to be seeing you Farley
bone find to contend with back pocket
I'd liberally apply it if
gumgum boat was a no good place
do I look like a machine on a sunny day?
stow that waitress dress
does it rain? does a snake?
a door over all this would help
pretty smart to even think
capstan mate on an unfired brick
brain tongues get silenced
there's a mutiny in this box
not ANGER anymore but DANGER
they forgot to grease up the tree
may have to report myself missing
just three grabs from the top
and I can see that
faraway look in your eyes

ZAPPER CLEANSE

I got angry poems
mystical bread pump poems
could I fuck you without repeating you?
the angle of the situation is to ditch
it's a monkey among the apes
a smith amidst the drivel
you have to take my arm I have no other
then the creature concurs or begins to
fall in
the medical poems
the laffable poems
the poems with a rubber for strictness
a kinship to the fucking residue
I have a problem for you

THESE ARE THE LOUDER DROPPINGS

Gout   Gort
tort   toast
supremas   subbrain
inky little hulk in bind
I'll take out an ad in the Brick Kiln Folio
green tinge to everything now will bother you
blinks and nods until it's hostile
but don't try to blanket me
the loosenings are starting to lateral
are you a fixed figure here in LaGovina?
I've had enough of your rigmarole
   (a small squat henna hen
    or bronze kickball?)
make a loop from your sun intelligences
and you'll have your answer
   (the Blackguardry of Demetrios)
but these new takeouts are a certainty
make your legs go the other way and we'll see
   (Dreshman is not hopeful)
just one of my toes came up in the mirror
send soon care of the Dulcet Sailor
   Afraid of Where It's Rising
     Genus Corps Patrol
       Atlantis
         (ping)

NARY AN OATER

Subcutaneous plumb bobs
restrung every evening
have left Airman Dan an infant
how do you measure bliss?

CHANCE MOVES OUT

Give me an absolutely square tomb
it'll save everybody time
possibly a Chinese time but anyway
we thought we heard something
waiting for the latest burn
a storm for lunch?
then the door came open on a silent car
here where the ears grow up
a flyswatter known as the GoGetter
a bread of the walls they speak of here
hot red domes of the terminal city
stretch and you form attachments
did they do it on a dare?
death is becoming cubical
the ends where they dent are not mentionable
in any place the paper snaps
make sure there's enough lead
in your clothes

BLOWN CUES IN WILD WOODS

A cannon full of grass on the Miser's Road
in fact this whole war is a pest
put that gun up your nose
sensible orders come from broken buildings
eating and raping at the time on a gelato mountain
were you born a mortician?
turned out an assault on a queen
don't worry about the show this is only a shower
girls with no clothes on the stairs
mud on their strings
drink from red gaps in the lining
now it's all Calcutta below ground
better take Captain Calypso on
a coffee venture brighter
than the beets on his mind
then Corporal Killer collapses overtaxed
the teats show and you won't be having
lunch in school anymore
shove the whole war into a cube
formed to brace it just there
just a larger than usual arranged death
and see that you count until you do

MOO GOO GAI PENURY

On the square the tanks shrieked like birds
Billie Wheatleigh held the fire pin out
no use plugging these edible gentlemen
"why those rounds are all batteries"
see the men heading into their own gaps
mudguards ahoy!   from the houses
from their blinds and sills
a coal mark above every hash point
"we'll be rolling them our boils next"
and scream into the winking sweater
a miracle the shits weren't taken
drilling up under the flood
are these machinery killers?
they're puddling enough
push on that lever
did you see the seat move?
a conflict decided by settled glances
remove your gum from the dome
do that woman out of her cheaters
risk every belly trouble
your hands will be crossed
as this vision ends

THE GILL ROWS TO NOWHERE

The crusted stamps on the bush wall
of this contraption still give
a faint heat
a vein plant
frightening and letting up
he has her whole life in this
femme at large
clean streets at last
a dog at the end of his tensile stench
vitamins hidden in a barn
this occurred in Haddam
on the River Built
in the summer of encaustic stages
when the landings were left to drop
your hand all sandy from the shining
penetration fading
to a sandstone stop
and all this fission still pending

CHEEP

Cora Lee banded the stones
it was Applemass and the stains
got lifted in a light grey pulse
was this Appointment Japan?
roaring momsas led with their tits
as her hand was just about specimen
at the gypsum heart of a transparent
actual living space
you see them run around in
tranquilizer pants
leaving tissues from here to Jeroboam
on the map of strange eons gone tacky
but we knew this and just as soon
as they got to sample height
Saddler's Wells were declared
now isn't that just spotty?
in a minute my mineral paint class
where they roll this over the floor
and fiddle with it then piddle on it
goes to show

CAUSE CAP'S THE LIMIT

In the wine glass deep
we removed the toggles from Betty Boop
now where's your coast guard sun?

A BANANA TUCK IN THE MOON (VARLET)

Just a bench mark on the romper road
coals glow to exhaust dust
shit on you
hey Eva! you saddle pumper
your pa just lost his band
but you run and I'll still love your seat
no plain window or Blanding's Dreamhouse
but
talking to the boy whose lamp jarred loose
that bird on the bridge suffered heart attack
Krakatoa spawned too many waltzes
eventually to arrive at your breath
drained off into Quasimodo's Villa
so take your drawing and lie down
my glands are all in beaverboard stereo
take down your sash weights and back into a push
his hash was made out of red plush
the brighter lights whenever you wink
or need some glassine pop
to cross the boards bounded in brown
my handwriting gone down with my pants
I need Red Herring Plummet Juice
a chair back green in the sun
in the shape of an eight
24 hours to every state
but this dream must be shown
in less than one week

HUEY LOUIE AND DEWEY ON EGGS

They're pathetic in their comber wickets
it's like keeping vitamins in your pants
we prefer oblong malts
a smatter of tags along cluttering paths
their purposes narrow
and spelt from a kit
they are too orange oranger not orange enough
we nearly got caught the last time
gnawing like tree goats and it was finished
our uncle had us marbleizing that
table till all the snow forts fell
the whole place an interior of tank
and we failed
no better than Chuglet Pops
never to gabble among
the closing papers again
now if only we had gone rich

LOW ON THE MONIKER
(IT ARRIVES IN WAVES)

Bruce Conner's Horn Flowers
and Horsecollar Burnett
and the words in the trees that
got shrinkwrapped
and the burning mystery at my stem
that don't you just know it
and burying the relics instead
the river coming up in my mind
well past the safety floor
and I see Bruce raise
an ivory handkerchief
and the men roll past
in Ziploc partitions
that we have come to the end of
our rocket condition
with needlenose phonographs
a totaling of the adherents
have you heard of this work of skull?
I've stood by long enough
I'll now destroy the brain
that made me come
lock up the window where
they harden things
whispering of the volumes that
can't be opened
and the crystals and the spice

THE DEROS

The Deros live way deep in
well machined apartments
and these are not experiments
they will have you when they want
every time you come they ratchet
you tighter
your mind is their familiar
so the race fails as they indicate
just ask Nick Diabase
sure there are steel doors in hills
you mustn't approach
and elevators you'd be a fool to
push the basement button again
but they've got it all in place
down to the last animalcule
and have had since
that December 1947 issue of
Astounding Magazine
where you see this guy . . .

A TREATER'S CROSSUPS

Baryshnikov had a sandwich
he sat on
telling the story of the tower
lanky and signed to the starfield
his name originally Marsh
of the Sheboygan Marshes
tellers of similar stories
friends in high places
cynosure of all eyes
but one has gone further from here
his name was Sanders and he fled
a life sentence awaiting
the inadequate answers
a grown man and a traitor
to the very air he breathed
the very tales he told
a plotter of magic stealth
tuner of molasses barrels
major of the corps ballet
for all anyone knew
a sort of monk-ape
you never know where
you'll find your next meal

WAYS TO FORM IN TIME (THE BLINKERS)

It said they thought we'd see what?
politics?
a barn snail at a paper sale?
multiple triggers to a precise point
below the city make this querying effect
copious liars down at City Hall etc.
they all come out
meet the same barbs
treat the same carbons
rarely is the body wallet
right about the casebook head
below the crust there are meeters
shakers and doers
the open and the close of it all
and on weekdays the timber snake
opens its vast
on the cobbles and the space
but that's a former case

AND THE LUNATIC ROTATE

A female Gielgud in black veil
descends the priory stairs
puts the head in lock
hookups for sale in the dark
lake after lake after you
have not seen these persons again
cleanse the pages
hold birds' nests for hours
read a book about a lamp
then put down those household breasts
close inside the bed inside her head
Gogol would have needed a drill
made the sounds within your skull
release the smoky blade
or a trial version of the Castle

OVERNOVEL OWLS BEARING DOWN

MotetBoy Schutt was one
of the blinder redeemers
rendered in half by the Barn Dream Press
they had their own avenue in those days
was called Parceling the Breeder
hope you can learn to overdetermine
your living stalls
fish in bursts till the timing dud
but the Boy wouldn't listen
they had highways in those days
purple person in a parrot suit
didn't wish to write this
and wouldn't except for
the load crusts of a salary
these prompters had left
there's not a dreary hope
tear-ass and salivating
down on the Boy
river with a tuck
just a woebegoner's luck
he left off living at the Military Towers
throwing in the milky towel
blinking into the past

EVERY DEEP HAS LOWER DEVELOPMENTS

Menendez refused the newly minted clams
I couldn't reach the pockets at my own waist
do you know what is written on
the bottom of this porringer?
try some glass wax
I wish I could relieve all the prelates
a drawbridge with a washroom awaits you
sick of all this relentless tempo
couldn't it well be lowered?
Gus Tongas supreme stumblemass
and out on the highway a frog leaps unknown
wishing on an elbow grown devious
all these extended devices
well, suit yourself
this stinks like a coppermine
let it come down
goodbye Froggy

SOME EARLY CANON

Guns that run
on a sort of powdered paraffin
a force of failures in lucite blocks
I have become arrogance itself
but I have not yet piled things further
enough
straight meats in silence
she wears a terrace in her bare broadness
more of the careful flasks to cast
to crown a fringe to eat
and file out west to gain lust
and the perfect hamburger
the flavor of mackerel
an adopted ivory branch of trim
gold leaf is all over my own ideal
where the silence is coated with leaves
and we will go and we will come
to high lands with muffled bones
as scary a crew as even I've seen
rolled into a rope of careful hobby
the winning of counterfeit dates
Islamic blocks
in the country of calcified clocks
and the separate snakes that thread them
to put out all the fires in a single day
and not touch the sword to the needle
where my brother is
my avenue for stuff broached
a couple of gaps in the sidereal seminary

now clutch me not
for in lack of light
who can you trust?
Charlie MacCarthy
lost even his hair

STRETCHED OUT TILL THE KNOWLEDGE STOPS

A thin greyish line bidden into
hills bushes even locomotives
has finished many men
you see the juices rolling out
and it's goodbye to man's beaverboard game
repeat or no paisley favor
many's the sender Wild Bill put under
all the substance in the eyes

I FOUND AN ELEGY

The man with the biggest Gorbachev
cancelled once he heard the Yeoman's Prayer
Boxwood the Elder entered the office
all the talc missing from his laces
as Barnacle dips the paper in headlines
the man with the shorter scalp
on one side is your father
gone nugatory crossing waters
the woman with the white top hat
and the seaweed gloves
enters Slack House
we have knowledge of boners
in certain shadow palaces
but it's over for the others of
all of them
snake shot contracting in the entry
or the side of your nose
I grew oddly calm as this one concluded
Joseph Conrad on the sky-blue waters

BACTINE'S FAMOUS FLAMEOUT

Linda Hamilton had gonads
the size of gods
and Charlie Sheen ant paste left
over from Mother
the most plastic passages in
White House history
playing elevator tag with egg
cream vestiges
hit all the buttons at once and
it brings you
a long lenser to take up your evenings
world with its edges has too many colors
the elusive lab-fancier returns to Eden
apologetic jacket and ham hocks
"don't read *books*"
as a lasso shakes up your ink TV
and there's nothing worse than balances
where surds are concerned
where motherfuckers are solvents
Linda has no assurance that
Charlie will meet with China
have you ever brindled a cola?
stop merging with my line of march
I'll bring the radio after supper

MUST YOU? (SAW)

Ask Cancer Boy just
what he waits for
in his Dumpty wire wheels
he's too round that's his fault
his smile all along
a seam on budgery
there are spelling tasks he missed
'cause his ma had him out at the lab
learning buddy breakage and bleary
Cancer Boy's thoughts are roomy
like paying mind to aluminum perimeters
a mass of penduloma down the line
tells a joke writes a tune
spruces up on penury
Cancer Boy loose in the nursery
down the pumpkin rows beyond thievery
he'll spend it in his beanie
perfecting mopery
but oh so cutlery
nobody lasts

STEAMBOAT SPRINGS FOR THE NIGHT 1965

Little Libby Plotnose was excited
there was nobody else on her roster
and if you think this is leading anywhere
you're wrong
bladders exploding needles in fishes
the whole camp gone linseed etc.
give me a hand with these windows
there's nothing in them further
I'll have to take this poem home
if you don't dare read it out
a radio that receives only rootbeer ads
smoke over average towns a grab-iron
ringing contest and other
situations attitudes impossibilities
and there's even more that I've lost
and so has she and now
so have you

APPORTIONMENT AND SUSPENDED ENDING

My earliest friend was a shortcase
then came the allegedness
Cry Me A River and the album cover
especially what it showed like angel food
and the comic thief took away from us
our lists
counted among his friends the frogs
but we outwove each other
face to available catchup desk
ever choose a Chalcedony Louie?
free to dispose of our ways at last
'cause after all it ends up
it's the Story of the House
not us no technofacility
practice your rug would you?
practice your sides of health
even sometimes on time
your end,
           Tad Lime

LOAD SOFT, HE MIGHT TUMBLE

The Brutality of Bent Axen
came to the fore
I saw his various comings
and powdered lead goings
far as the Machinery River
is this the one you would bow to
be bloated by?
yassuh!
no throat about it
I'll become a mile sailor
and deep the dusks
or crop flying discs
in dead folks' dreams
a good lot of water has passed
since that husk of a deed
beyond which no cat has wandered
and now the excitement
but all in encasement
hey, Bent!

PLUS NINE LINES OF FEAR

Sylvia Pojoli gets kind of hysterical
when you mention her secret hairnet mines
deep in the national confidence
the principles of grock then squawk
maybe a whole brain storm
could come off in your hand?
but these walls are consumed in vesicles
and no one will heat my thoughts
before the glimmering of the time
give me a car a lamp and savagery
slide on down the hammer tree
and I'll seal you a velocity
there is a silence here and you
won't like it if I grow on
this nervous scent till dawn
signing off, SP
suiting up for everybody

MORE HELPINGS OF THE VITAL ROSTER

Send for Arbogast
he's good with stairs
feed Mary Worth her morning oats
hire Haaken Kalm
a dumb waiter
be a participator
look on the other side of Sidle Ridge
there is Harvest Vest
bright in the dawn
his clothes laid out in the night
so he won't have to fight
Dick Barthelmess for the dream
call One Arm
he's good for it
as if a chair chain was set
get Bone Drain Chet
leaving all the slaughter out
turn a radio spout
then a frogger with a net
a housing for these beans and the next
socket throat of Mel Dram
be a muter of the clam
put some charm in your claims
set your room on the world full of fiends
clamors claps and comets will rise
Velma and Waddo Sideshoe to surmise
Wattlebow and the Pawnees of Structure
Endbuckle Voit
Occipiter List

and the Dread Boys
now will you fill my bill?
clip my noise?
'cause it's not quite cozy in here

OF THE BRIGHTER BUYER

My head is on fire
it's the engines in there
gullible aren't you?
a residue of Donovan's Reef
plattersfull and dustbowls of rest
then I step right up to the card
then I sign an Ode to Garland
Beverly not Judy
scars and bars
that military dent
it's possible to keep a watch on your head?
what's the price on God?
closing time at Bubble City
but I'm not a joiner
carry all my planes in a net bag
mouth like a cotton coffin
spider flakes all up my back
I'm in a spot
a hole
the fire went out
that rockhard soy sauce gave me
blood in my alcoholic system
then I hit the ceiling
and the windows go chocolate prisms

WITH THE PLASTICITY OF FOOLS

You go up and down through
cut banks in the coal measures
a steaming trestle behind Hope High
it's the old neighborhood with
overlay new corridors in
the old vast hotel
and you go through and you know it
with Barbieo and Celia and
it's a close shave
but I haven't got the key
'cause I'm naked

GONE OVER

Backyards with iron
and lemon sun
the gradient sidewalk
I'm out in it
hum heat and differ
the baby is in the basin
behind the glare glass
ball and rockyard smash
noontime sifts
later for the books
the insects are nomads
plain as I palm my head
the war is over and
the neighbors are dead

GLAD TO SEE YOU STANDING

Chop chop señora
there are hats
and then there are sizes
true rows of the downcast face
you put them on over your shoes
a penetration brightly to be acknowledged
the planet around your ankles
in fealty to the rank sun
I went to dowager school
where the dragons molested themselves
it was downbeat futurific
furry with clusters of thermite fasteners
in cloisters of the Luck of the Duck
but we are far from shelving here
how is your display?
not so alarming in your head?
now I must waltz on
but when will it end
and what is the harm?

SHORT OF NOWHERE

Shouts
let me see your gun
your tongue
your gum
there can't be any reason you'd refuse
Byron's down for a physical
so why not ease your bulk?
shoes will be shined by the rising sun
your foes shown up as fools
is the timing wrong?
why these high-waisted waiters?
not a one with knowledge of the food?
show me something
come down off the faux heights
be a savior and peel me a dream
show me your drum here
the truth is a bone
sheer that stops

TABS ON GLITTER

Epidotes make a fine salad
but your Iceland Spar has rocks in it
trouble on the Table of Elements
a little coughing at the back of the hill
only brains here in belljars
heights of the mayonnaise tax
and the termination of a close history
now just unhook that dress
hum into the crystallized brandy
and we'll discuss the secrets of locality

ONE SHAPE RETURNS

Bob Conservatov
the bobbler of growth
enters the Overdome
wobbling
he's come to hate
the man monkeys jumping
So&So to Simplestorm
stop him before he pimples the realm
troubles in mind
his whichaway erratic jacket
has him pound at Alarming Farm
and too soon it's too late to stay out
the horrors and rogers and
tangles rot hard in his meat
turns out he comes on
sure as your masterwinker
bald as the banner slave
wide white times, eh Bob?
simple straight weirdest tenseness?
tongues in bolas
churns to stake the snake?
Bob
turn on your rent-a-stop tippytoes
frown on the spot
then leave

RHONDA FLEMING AT THE MEDICINE BUILDING

Nice and cold around the heart
the one around the block
hung over from the head
to the neck
where they walk alone
with lit legs
and folding doors
there's this heel's apartment
and then there's this
wall with the image of a frame
yank the pull and drop that butt
the slats are closing in
Mitchum crosses the room
in a trench and hat
never missing a timing
then the phone rings
like a brick with nowhere else to go
there were a lot fewer numbers
in those days
now let's just shrug off all
this ectoplasm
well, nobody can *help* it
or they get by with nothing but
a light a coat and a double
I must be slipping
this one's getting sort of burned up
I always say everybody's right
thunk it and brought it and bore it
let's not get lost in all this traffic
I stood there as long as a world

LIGHTS ONLY THE ONE TIME

The Bad News Birds have arrived
this coin-op morning
better pad your bible with
bike pumps and other feetsy trash
I made it about as far as the vestibule
then ack ack
overcome by own spit
let's try instead
bottom drawers
match stands and heresy
ever met Harry Hersey?
put the blinders back on the phone
and catch the Early Ernie Show
the Castoffs of Pituitary Island
or maybe the Lost City of the Anchors?
or maybe just
forget it

MOTHER TO MOUNT MY TREE

And yet I think she will straighten all of my things
out. Threaten with vulgarity the kinds that last
us good. The parishioner's face falls out.
There are claims.

And so I suppose to have used up all the fresh
words in my quiver. Holden Caulfield carefully
intrudes. A Parisian face with metallic blue
border. Grass that cuts like glass. Words that pop
and fall apiece.

Stop walking in the corridor while I'm in the room.
The table there is only for faltering. The jam jar
has rejected a close visit, close as a tram car.
Legs Larry MacDonald descried all reason, attempts
upon which had wholly taken his youth. Meanwhile
room a shade of lipstick now gone.

An epigone, look it up. She would soon march forth
and take over and then my life would begin to appear
in high relief. Particles for the guns. Aloof
as approaching a parlor. Good. I'm. Done. Even the roof
of the matter has gone. Plus this.

Going over my life with a fine-tooth mouth I find
nothing portable. A raisonné without gentians.
She rakes my voice like a map. Inside there is a room
set aside for avoidance. Pay the bank. Return to
the Lollapalooza you missed.

A lobotomy of lobstermen this time around and
the bookstore winner lights out for some spacial
countries. Seraglio with acne. A boar with dogs
on it. Freddie had a temper oh had he then. You'll
find a few lavender plates and what could the monster
do in there? The Mysterious Pennies of Bulk Inclusion.
I'd be stupid enough I'd found a school.

Give them the brick treatment. Open up a can for
the Palookas. Drink SNORD. She can always return
to revive me. Hobnail or no Shantung. I appropriate
the opal of no special dimensions, torque applied to
snail as big as a hippodrome. This is really supper.
When Dazzle was called the world we had pretended
foundered. Like she always says.

LAWN LAWYER HEAVEN

Black lacings on your spats bring
homosonorous blurtings out
over all you have to pay the day to be
or it's your style to fudge
a part in the revenant dulls
I'd have a care toy if I were pure
the Washington Indians patrol
the Beacon Edge Walkies
for ever and a ducket
then you roll it out flat and
pretend to take your fill
it's the Neighborhood of the Blendies
but we were ready for them
the day the industry came
down to a pencil
and the Pope let down his rope and
race dolls were formed
I'd take Alaska
only most of the beams are broken
the lights all out for a laugh
(some of my own disasters)

INTO THE GUM AGAIN AND HE'S MEAN

There's a bond guy inside me
wants my wonder years
but Bronx cheers bum steers
or near beers he'll need
to settle for
anything that rhymes with
the present contagion
I made myself head of the squadron
put the man on notice on the moon
now in these neighborhoods the storms
have personalities
conic sections and Mylanta
by the bucketload
so I tell the bound one
not to air his doubts
this is the course of history
rife with depressive contents
longer than a blindman's breath

EVERY MAN JACK CHEWS IT OVER (GREEN)

Maybe I'm a hyena
and all my friends make bubbles underwater
squid cause heart attacks
rig for depthcharge
I have let the strings dismay me
lead me into another role as "Chooch"
I mean have you seen through
these windows?
just let the colors keep you down
watch the bookends sink
at the end of the trouble there is
a parallel loginess
but to test a "gravid lens" you need
actual conditions
blap bloop
when I asked Ernie Borgnine about this
century he said "hop"

GULP

Do you see that building behind us?
the tiny inhabitants land on actual brains
all the very hands have been wiped away
Doctor Mooncell here higher than any window
but three boners later
the meaninglessness of clothing in the face of
too many beings dreaming of the sun wind
the nuts and bolts of battle
all in a book titled Granite in Toto
Edward Dahlberg banished beyond Pluto
"just get over it, sweaterhead"
do these dolphins want the baloney to arrive?
recalcitrance the key to connectivity
you turn over and over in your sleep
a shakiness of the tonal hemispheres
but is this the way to probe death?
candied lights in long dark rooms?
code name Bladder Tribes
now there's a new use for all these worlds
let the Gummy Bears bear me
out

THE GUNSEL LOSES
(SET YOUR PHASERS ON DISTURB)

He descended the pot on a length of rubber flex
a mistake
and so died enmired in graham cracker paste
to a depth of forty meters
"beyond this point I have not liked to go"
cut off at the throat
if was foggy in those hills
there are the ones that have to glue
their hair to their scalps
take a tuck in their abilities
Hogan Gofers we called them
but the skull in the basin
"I did not regard with a cheerful aspect"
or the point at which he ducks
the coming ledge but misses
these are the soiled thoughts
of a potter who works in
psilomelane only
egregious pumper of the viscid lair
a coughing treatment on its last legs
a sort of golf violin
its hairless digits remain damp
but you know and so you go
"swift away this place from"
stuffed space of murmurs
a palace of tumors?

I BLEW EISENHOWER'S DICK OFF

Put too much salt in my punctuation
spent too long with the Bunkum Fiddlers
ending on a pall
or was it a rattler's pull?
coughed and went away
am I a liar?   didn't I ever
drill your pecks?
make a living of you
a puddle for your love?
but at least it was mad
Eisenhower came encased so
had to be cracked loose
up in the Elephantine Boonies
that day the crusts turned back
rehearsed to a paling tone
an awful lot of coffin on my shoe
then up at Northern Bolt it's learned
that I'm okay but he's not

SURGERY IN FRIENDS

Wait here for a festival
hearts of rash depths of dull
a real priest does not know
his numbers
a ghost with no notion
of a wracking cough
God hear my shovel through
the centerboards of heaven
harken to my bloody waste
the sun shining on the water
is mean
glubglub went Eigner down the edge
of his fasting poem
it's too hot to know
any names well
gargoyles have grown through my soup
listen!
you might have stopped all this
before reaching Moray Virginia
but no, you had to have stopgap eyes
a mustache out of a chimney
and cerulean damps
so welcome to Cue Gardens
where the Gimps

ON THE PROD

Implausible how Brannigan came late
gave 'em the slip
the born cheater
he was a saw doctor
based around Bone Line
where the Watchers
an open organ outlet?
close onto Lava River
Sand City?   there are no barbers
only a chocolate sky
at the whim of a barn burner
"was I wrong, Miss Worth?"
it's a boon all this leaning on rivers
but I spose you knew that
like cake the snot
off my holding home
it's a bone quirk
this rage for dusk
a classic habit grown too large
too ripe on vast gas flats
"Occupiers don't rattle me"
the situation is a nut
I wouldn't take that
on a bet   SNAP
hood ornament there
vaulted into my future
so hold this over
high on Death Ridge
almost till the clock's

FLAVOR OF THE MOUTH

Tragacanth
awkward fistula
lame lake
Arcturus sending
give me all your bread
article on the tiny bell
so-so man all tied
vomit in place
average dodo
short snort though pestered
viburnum to the thigh
awk awk Mister Masticator
magician with hollow calf
blows to come to
angle length legs
bulk sighs
that gum came out
through the brainstem
man

BAUXITE ON THE BOOKS

Halfmast taxonomy will last you nearly
to the patent end
that and rock olives in a mattress
you can be sure of
ever read Mallory?
I had nine dimes as a child
now I have bubkes (potlatch)
ever have a melon receive
the cross of crystal teeth?
Augmented Man steals down the street
has too much to rhyme at
last to be a sand soldier
and farm his corns in the shade
of a tenement pole
broadcast to all but Henry
who bothers

DRAW ME A SHORT DEER

I walked out on my self
but missed the ledge
a testimony to nylon
dorks talk in cars
starve like crows
if that's any sample
some of these rocks
looks like you could eat
former stringer down a street
hit a rattler bump?
try Remegel
thought I had no more timeouts
but here's a day's water
how long does it take to
try Fred Hersch?
zounds! poison dirt
"throw my man a hen"
got my slingshot pistol crutch
said it was a crystal botch
meanwhile I've got my hand mine
now to color that sewage
mostly feldspar anyway
I'll believe that when I break it
now if I can only stop
falling back in
smell that door stop?
Robert Ryan says I might even live

MAMACITA POPS A LIGATURE

The stork waddler was put on peptides only
pep tones those little shill rods so snubby
fill you with potryzebie windings?
not sure those tiddly road pampers
old jobs?   know your reptile
rhyme awhile before you wake
take a cork and hone a weapon of it
drain lake and later the cops'll watch you
got any further couplings?   lobster poles?
alerts worthy of the Land of Adhesives?
I like to see the Germ Men warring
but whose leg of this trip'll align you?
me I make out stories
the sooner the tree lips catch
the more the furor

THE SNEEZE IN PROFILE

Pianissimo Death
was an Organism Beast
had a store-bought odor
grew alarmingly
then in his wake
came the Varlets
Apassionata von Crematoes
Presnell Bindlefarther
and Vulva the Land
all form a grunt base
a tagalong on sticks
a lava form integral
with the loose dough
but just enough drag
that the raisins shift
downward but separately
toward the edges with
the cloth dark glass
you'll see just the hand
when this Sifter rules

BUTTER UP YOUR ENTROPY
WHILE THE SMILES ARE FREE

I've lost confidence in my rag
the one I put between thought and reason
and the nightmare maneuvers of
Heimlich whimsey
some call it cheese but
I call it cutting
the way the breath revolves in the chest
I have to call Joe Anthropos
the keeper of gospel fossils and various
bell glamour
no doubt I'll relent and let
the garnet heads flake
pull in no light
shut off the bulbous
and see him streak
the one so fast he even lost his hair
in the grim trust of process
past the Tower of Kimbo
am I gone beyond number?
now where's my weapon?

THE METAL PETALS' CREAMY REACH

Christ, Ontkeans!
bobular little drivel boys
hitching up the tide
reaching like they died
balls tied to their neverendings
the gyre was on the snow
blonde with soap
and the vital waders
do you hear a snore?
this scow has met the clitoral limits
humming in a bow
hurrying till a fill of snarls
is gotten by all and Remley
Brindlematey the Stored
I marked all their cards with keys
shining off the shelf
the one with the post
do I hear a barely snarfled laughing?
put on your toad
take the liar's lead
sure is deadly down the totaling

LIKE A KNEEFLEX

Barbells are my nasal codes
start with blood you end on a list
megaphones and dermatitis
consider the Limestone Greeks
not even change for
an errant bus locker
wish I had the hand to do it up
to wing those big wheel tires
this time it was sedimentary
to smile only in books
the joke it was former
more than trouble at the bubbler
left like a message at the tone

BRANIAC ON BANJO

Sal Hepatica had a dream
the world would be run on serpentine
hushabye don't you rise
the man lifts his tenor and so he digs
an orange rocker on a leaden porch
and you get three visits
Turnkey Aileron and Wiseguy
draw a new nose for the songbird
as half a calendar accordions in
we get to trying people for
their habits not their failures
ain't that a peach?
now face the wall and descend
make old mangy Parbat eat his words

IN BRUCEMAN'S BATTERYWAY

It's like robbing the cradle
of those colored beans
the Arbutron numbers show how
your horses take their places
in this ingrate rain
la la la the housing comes clear
on that point anyway
that the city may die in a sulk
of smoky tans and wanes
then I got to work in a habit barn
on the last of the inkworm savages
it's a testimony to the commonplace that
when things grow loose and empty
you see the entryway girl twist
her stems fragile and come down
do you think you'll last?
make your way despite
the steel sleeve monolithic hooters?
this is a gasworks
and this is how it piles
no shit as long as no one
comes home to the pelagic fist
death in centipede
and all the slogan murmurs are in tempo
a sort of plasmic agitation
here we have the world's slowest dangers!

TELL ME ONE THING

Do you accept Jay Foo Flood
as your personal bearer?
do you take any old god as
your assigned apparatchik?
do you accept Sheena
as Queen of the Jungle?
do you grunt every time you
bang the window?
are these definite feelings
as freeing as what you feel
in your Lincoln County jacket
or rub-down car coat?
I say
dumber questions have never
been whittled
so press Prevention
on your Burroughsian former
show some sand

TRYING

Guy named Blostylston had it set up
so he could watch everything as he
pictured it. Made an end-lunge around
the whole population while his eyes
behaved as sadly as Plourdes. Don't
you see? His eyes became important.
The rest was all chartreuse singers
and girders of the blood. The powers
that blew. Finally all he wanted was
to give the real Plourdes (now grown
to a knighthood) a fully-equipped
laboratory and then slip out at midnight
on the terminal lurk. I have seen this.
I reek with having seen. Make of it
what you can find to do.

CUP RINGS

The bell sounds and then
you're let out to sleep
there's a peel
stop dreaming of mass shampoos
the wagons to have you on
to mock up grins
in back like a pluperfect rift
in smegma research
really get to know your knob
the shine on this fool now
has attentively nothing to do with you
after all the sadness
passes so quickly like a doorway
the shift is coming unplumbed
time to practice your diretissima
time to break a smile
time to time your waste
'cause time will take your face
these flecks of time and space

BACK IN THE TIME OF THE TUBE

I beeped at myself suddenly
alarms going off out of hair
and the light in bald hot taste
scarfing compasses to the waist
table chapters with no care
the fat man wanted to eat his
shoes then the bulb
well it goes dry
white slab and I'm ashamed
gunk
that's all
just gunk and phenomena and phoneboxes
give me a solid dime for the tap
of my fat white hat
zombified
beyond any last request

TRAPPED IN A NAZI STOOP

I saw the bombs go off like my sighs
I used to be bigger
now I go to Hofstra
would you give me a jiggle?
the French gets caught in my throat
gobbed
then held the boarding line
have they sent the buckling word?
there are lumps in this bee
send it back
just stay on the blimp roles
we can still be eaten
like Bobbies on the Superchief
I'll set up an onion row
then let the Blurries blow it down

NOT OH

Plutarch releases a helium balloon
partial armistice in cellophane hands
this planetary nun with paper on her head
runs dead by dubious morning
twas a lead paper
when you're dying you ask for another
"but he asked for some more"
fuck off! crows Billy Haverstack
it's time to tie your classics in knots
else get up a blue head of plasma
bag of tongues bag of towels
the lying goes down in tropes
bent now to include
a totally feldspar hill they make pencils of
tight fist but no sobbing
and a bloody tunnel for all your
emotional trading

ARE YOU ASHAMED OF YOUR SULFUR?

Plaid dead that's what
Bucky Bug eating gravel till he's randy
as Americans puff their surfboards
and I put in tacks
try bringing out the chocolate kits
play Murray Worries His Samples
stop
start the quest for a name for
your sister the one who's on land
stop
all occupation has stopped
nothing but a red herring high
stirring in the steeper worlds
now can Death be brought to nothing?
say what?
the Endeavor Bug has his ballhead on
but will not speak

OUTWARD TILL YOU DUCK

On a fire escape with a searchlight
we don't move from that place
equal stools and flooded mattresses
places where things are laid in Arabic
a flaking buttress of ball twine politicians
grasp it in the old gold ground
the casted extended rebels fancy
something goofus and festered and you know
the oncologists listened leaning flueward
I'd have to set you up differently
heck of a fellow settling for dust
in basic dad
let's bury all those who would carry
Nelly Young in stages and settings
for words a hogshead of a good time
the Beanball Raiders have asked me here
over all your possible coin-operated
objections once again and now on since
brigandry is not husbandry
like a lock is not a miss
and I go at rates
beyond the ruse of substitute
I'll never kiss the girls
press like an alligator no
never work as regulator
but probably end on a sigh

MEN WITHOUT LABELS

A long pair of pliers so what's with the Pleiades?
crying a whole lot in glasses
are you going to collapse my crack?
I have this aluminum burnish on my head
and you're practically fragrant
the story of a wallrat
on paper there's no turning back
to front a grave-robbing operation
why me?   in the sun
burning trees like Herakles
we forgot about that Abner dude
with the baldass brother goofy
take it to Walgreen's
nonsense there *is* no living
stay private means own an iron lamp
and keep your dogs out of the wind
I wear the papers like Batman
loves his cape or a jazz octet
or the psycho licks a lightbulb
blocked by tension at the temples
think I need a hobby trying heat washers
these streets are something
though totally lacking in grace

OTHERS

Boys with boils in their eyes
see newts by the sun wick
a hornet in my opportunities
planning rehearsal death
aslant in the prong weathers
I have seen where the stairs turn rash
to the enclosure of the mint toad
you dim wick
stubs its fin in darkness
only pretend to dress
rehearsing a wineman's glaring independence
and to think I doubted my appendages
ugliness in puzzle rooms
running patterns on a wind's reverse
give me my planet back!
you'll see it glisten and I won't know you
the trouble with people is blood

IN MEMORY OF THE UNDEAD

Blades are for diamonds
noodles for the uncaught
star field for your next blind thought
only to be found mumbling
night from the day
the cobras from the trees
look out any window
you'll find syzygy
and that blond dairy snake Henry visits
there are voluntary passages
and then the Purple Onyx Highway
for gingerbread and balladry
the waiting part of husbandry
first of several novel thoughts
the rest away diminish
to a barrel roll futurity
but luckily it's said
you landed on your head

DARLINGS BOUND

Great asphalt portions of the tale
are left by the wayside
silly people that are pretty but
I was in love with the most
beautiful assumption
Brandenberg ugliness and a sprite
lived on Wayland Avenue with a popsicle
burning braziers for religious defensiveness
then the liquor hit the bell
the Legend of a Really Big Head in the Street
and now everyone's pretending that all this
dust is fuel
coprolites under glass
bull
but it's fine
shocked at his own suggestion
and now there's too much red on the block
bones and the talk of hacks
no goal is pretty
they say she loves me anyway
he has a crippling influence
Men and Women Behaving Badly
this should have been called

LIKE THE BLISTERS ON A PIECE OF CHAMPAGNE

The silence of the shadows is deafening
squirt me a bloom of water
substance
or park it in a black hole
Keith Mustache leads to a car
this fabulous speck on the earth's surface
where the cabbage grows alarming
and tomorrow the syrup reaches
the spaghetti factory
we'll all learn to live with barbells
spanakopitta not to your liking, señor?
the name will be Cochran till this story's done
now give me the president of Sorghum College
or let some water out of the lake, one
it's too late for circumference
and whatever you do don't
return to my knowledge